Absolute Zeal

Absolute Zeal

The A, B, C's of Joy

Toni Nanette Menard

ABSOLUTE ZEAL
THE A, B, C'S OF JOY

iUniverse books may be ordered through booksellers or by contacting:

iUniverse
1663 Liberty Drive
Bloomington, IN 47403
www.iuniverse.com
844-349-9409

Because of the dynamic nature of the Internet, any web addresses or links contained in this book may have changed since publication and may no longer be valid. The views expressed in this work are solely those of the author and do not necessarily reflect the views of the publisher, and the publisher hereby disclaims any responsibility for them.

Any people depicted in stock imagery provided by Getty Images are models, and such images are being used for illustrative purposes only.
Certain stock imagery © Getty Images.

ISBN: 978-1-6632-0873-6 (sc)
ISBN: 978-1-6632-0874-3 (e)

Print information available on the last page.

iUniverse rev. date: 09/19/2020

I dedicate this book to those friends and family, near and far, that have shared and created joy with me.

Absolute

The Absolute is truth. Truth, while solid, in a romantic dichotomy, wisps around one's legs to bolster them up. To find joy, embrace joy, we must hold on to the absolute truth like a lifeline. For truth is the key in finding your way to everlasting joy. The sun rises and sets, as does the moon in the opposite. The constant of this is the cornerstone to your joy.

Belief

We each have our own sense of knowing, of realization. Whether it be about what color we prefer, to the best name for our first child. What it is we hold dear in thought are our own special beliefs. These personal beliefs encompass you and define who you are. You must have faith in your own, resonating truth to follow the call to joy.

Care

To care in general means that your heart is open. This is critical for joy to slide in. A softened heart may mean we cry at movies, but we also cry when someone reaches a momumental goal; even our own. We are glad to be of help to others, just as we care for ourselves. This special caring is a caveat to joy's blossom.

Dream

Dream big, dream small, but dream. As we think on those things that nurture us and bring us gladness; our path to joy is paved. Sometimes the idea of dreaming is "something out of reach", but dreams are there to come true daily. Is not a blue sky a dreamy miracle in and of itself?

Evolve

Oh to grow and change; both fearful and a truth. The secret is to keep the best of growth and change, let that fester, and cut out that which does not serve you. You will instinctively know what enriches you and enables a high-flying state of being if you're aware of your evolvement. That is what the passing of time brings to us; a better self.

Frame

Our view of thngs is a choice we have. Sometimes very difficult, but we have the choice to see different aspects of the same event or same circumstances. It is how we frame this event in our mind that makes the malleable truth. Ebenezer scrooge comes to mind, as he went through a major transformation by re-framing his reality. He was callus and cold, and through the sight of reality, he was able to find gratitude, a soft heart and ultimately a joyful exuberance.

Grace

The reverence of grace keeps your heart soft. A soft heart is open to caring and ultimately the receiving and giving of joy. Grace is angelic, as it is soft and pure like a child's first smile. This purity brings upon us an honest sweetness.

Heed

Heed your instincts. Your gut is always telling you your deep-most truths. What heeding is, is following your soul's innate impulses, and trusting what those may be. Heeding in yourself is both recognizing and following your personal path.

Inspect

All along your path to joy, take stock; notice. Have you fallen off course? Are you full-steam ahead loving, caring and full of faith? Inspect your insides and outward place in life. Inspect others, trust your gut so you will always recognize truth; from yourself and others.

Jolly

The word itself sounds like what it means: in good spirits, happy; to be convivial among people and to be lively, merry and cheerfully festive.

Kind

To be kind causes a warmth to well up inside yourself. It actually causes change in the world. To exercise being kind, can bring you riches; the most of those being joy.

Loyalty

Be loyal to your heart first and foremost. Beyond that, give your loved ones your loyalty. It is a gift you give yourself. To be loyal is a strength that has deep roots that keep you solid in this massive population. A loyal person is trusted and moreover, loved.

Malleable

The press pull of change is necessary to be alive. It is important to believe in the need for change, when it is called for, and not hold too tight to something that is long past true and good. Be adaptable or shapeable in mind body and soul. The ability to move with the winds of change brings truth and joy.

Nurture

Think of a tiny puppy, when it first joins your home. You want to pet it, feed it the appropriate food, with a treat or two. You have an instinct to nurture this puppy with love and kindness. We know this is how to make them behave for one, and be happy which the joyful part is. Nurture your friends and loved ones and even those you work with. You will get nurtured right back.

Obey

Obey the tenants of heartfelt consciousness. Obey those things that are right and good. Follow ones heart but in addition, do what is right for others. To heed ones gut, you will know joy by this giving.

Patience

Oh the waiting, and this is a truth. Sometimes times are stagnant and stopped. Muster up your patience and times will evolve into movement. There's a lovely saying, "There's Joy in the Morning." I take it to mean, we always have the gift of a new day and changes with it.

Quest

Life is a quest. I think it is safe to say, we mostly quest for happiness. Joy is an exalted version of happiness. Keep your eye on the path that will lead you to your happiness. Move toward it. Like in sports when you keep your eye on the ball, keep your quest clear in front of you. You will arrive at your happiness.

Respect

A gift every living person deserves is respect. We are questing toward happiness together, albeit at our own pace. We want and deserve respect ourselves, and it is important to surround yourself with those who give you that. Your path will be fortified as such.

Stillness

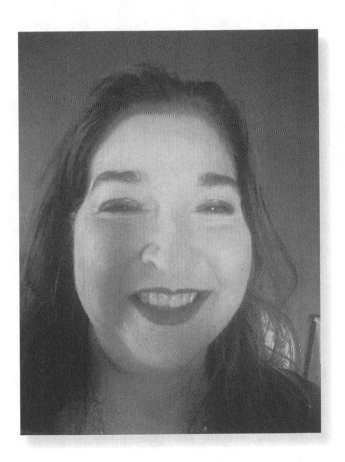

Meditation is a lofty word, truly just meaning to be still. Take the time for this stillness to reflect and know you are on your path to joy and happiness.

Temporal

We are but temporary majestic creatures of light living in temporary bodies in a temporary life. In this unknown slice of time, we experience much, good and bad. To grasp this is a way to live fully and with a positive outlook. Anything can happen, the best can come your way. We reap what we sow, meaning that which we give out into the world is what we create to come upon us. And, we have a finite time to create our joy.

*U*nderstand

Knowledge is power and a useful kind. It helps us get the job we want, it helps us converse in a cohesive way and it opens us up to ideas and inspiration. Seek to understand and your life will widen and bring more.

#

Your voice and thoughts must ring with integrity. All that you speak and stand up for must have the purity of integrity behind it. Integrity is the truth in you; the same place joy bubbles up from. Integrity is the fortitude you possess. It is the stellar honesty of a person. To vocalize always with integrity brings joy in the truth that integrity is.

Will

The will of a person is the bounty of strength one possesses. With that bounty, our voice develops, as in self and expression therein. With a strong will we can accomplish anything we set out for, and create and receive all the joy we desire as it is endless in its magnitude.

Xylose

Xylose is a sweet substance derived from corn. I use this to speak of the sweetness in you. In each of us is innate kindness, sweetness and a true and fine nature. All the sweetness you share, comes back toward yourself in multitudes. It spreads like caramel and sugar syrup. Shared sweetness is caring, sharing, pleasure and…joy; all attributes we seek are already with our heart in Life.

Yes

Affirmations are a way to give oneself big bolsters all day long. It is necessary, no, imperative that you believe in yourself. Joy follows that mindset.

Zeal

Eager desire and excited diligence is zeal. There is exuberance and ardor aplenty when you are touched by zeal; in general or for a person or idea. That is joy. Excitement aplenty. It is yours for the taking; with a little work.

Printed in the United States
By Bookmasters